B-COMING

MY JOURNEY FROM
BOYHOOD TO MANHOOD

KEVIN D. BOUDREAUX

FULL BLOOM PUBLISHING

B-Coming: My Journey from Boyhood to Manhood
Copyright © 2018 by Kevin D. Boudreaux
www.KevinDBoudreaux.com

ISBN: 978-0-9852839-3-3

Published by: Full Bloom Publishing

No part of this book may be reproduced or transmitted in any form
or by any means without written permission from the author.

For more information contact:
Full Bloom Publishing
13189 Veterans Memorial Dr. #91
Houston, Texas 77014

O: 1.855.62BLOOM
www.lifeinbloom.org

Book Project Management:
The Master Communicator's Writing Service • www.mcwritingservices.com

Cover and Interior Design: D.E. West / ZAQ Designs

Printed in the United States of America

All Rights Reserved.

FULL BLO✻M PUBLISHING

DEDICATION

To my earthly **Father Lawrence Boudreaux**, I am so glad you and I could find closure and enjoy our last few days together. Father's Day 2009 is a day I will always cherish. Love You and Miss You!

To my **Mother, Evelyn J. Boudreaux** Thank you so much for always standing in the gap for me! Thank you for being the Influence that helped me to become the man I am today! I am the man I became because of the way you raised me. Your actions are a true testament of Proverbs 22:6 (Train up the child in the way he should go, and when he is old, he will not depart from it). Mama, in coming up I may have lost my way but what you taught me has never and will never depart from me. Thank You JB! I love and miss you dearly! #LOOKINGUP

CONTENTS

Dedication iii
Foreword vii
Acknowledgements ix
Introduction xi

CHAPTER 1: B Intentional 1
CHAPTER 2: B Forgiven 5
CHAPTER 3: B Strong 9
CHAPTER 4: B You 19
CHAPTER 5: B Free 23
CHAPTER 6: B Consistent 33
CHAPTER 7: B Disciplined 47
CHAPTER 8: B Confident 51
CHAPTER 9: B Coming 67

About the Author 73

FOREWORD

B-Coming: My Journey from Boyhood to Manhood is a timely book indeed. With what we are facing in our nation, this book is so needed. Many of our boys are growing up without fathers for one reason or another. Unfortunately, they don't have grandfathers or uncles to step in and take the place of their fathers as role models. It is time for the men of God to arise and stand in the gap. The roles of women (be it mothers, grandmothers, aunts, etc..) are important, however, there are things that a woman just cannot teach boys when it comes to *becoming* men.

Author, Kevin D. Boudreaux gives his personal testimony on his journey to becoming a man hoping to help boys and men not make the same mistakes he made. He even addresses the fact that some men, now in adulthood, may still be in the state of becoming because they never dealt with issues of their childhood.

B-Coming: My Journey from Boyhood to Manhood gives sound practical advice and encouragement on how to handle being a man and everything that comes with it. It addresses such topics as finding God and allowing Him to be the head of your life, being a man before and after marriage, and being the Father your children need you to be.

This book is designed to and will help you walk in purpose, for purpose, and on purpose as you become the GREAT man God has ordained you to be.

Dr. Connie Stewart
Master Life Coach, Bloom U

ACKNOWLEDGEMENTS

To my Lord and Savior Jesus Christ, thank You for Your Unconditional Love and Sacrifice! You loved me when I didn't even think I was worth loving! And for that, I am eternally grateful.

To my Loving, Caring and Supportive wife Darla, thank you for always being there. No doubt it was and has been your prayers and support that has helped get me this far. I am honored and thankful that I get to share this accomplishment with you! #teamus #teamboudreaux 1*4*3

To my daughters Shariye, Ke'Bria and Shania, I hope that this will be a testament to the three of you that there is nothing you can't do. If you put forth the hard work and dedication toward any goal you can achieve it! I strive at doing my best as a father so that in return it would motivate you ladies to be and do your best! I pray I have made and will continue to make you proud! Love You!

To Patrick, Cherry, Gregg, Jaunta, Chastity, Sadie, Marcus and Derrick "The Niners", thank you for what you guys have done for me over the years. And remember no matter what to always Look-Up!

To my writing coach Sharon Jenkins, We Did It!!!! I could not have done this without the deposit you made in me to make this book not just a seed but an actual birth! Thank You for all your help! I have delivered my first book baby! And I couldn't have done it without you being my midwife/coach. #push

To my Pastor, my Spiritual Mother and my Life Coach, Dr. Connie Stewart, you saw this in my pathway before I saw it in myself. And because you know what God showed you, you refused to allow me to be nothing less than what God called me to be. Thank you for your prayers, your leadership and the shove when I needed it!

INTRODUCTION

As you awaken, you will come to understand that the journey to love isn't about finding "the one", the journey is about becoming "the one"!

– Creig Crippen

The day was September 30, 2016. I was sitting in a meeting with my Life Coach and we talked about how God is our Father and how we should trust Him just like we want our kids to trust us. And once she said it, I had to ask, "Well, what if you could never trust your father?" POW!!! When I said it, the feeling that came over me was a complete surprise. Something inside me leaped, and I immediately began to tear up. I even had to excuse myself and went to the restroom where the tears flowed uncontrollably. I cried like a baby!

I did not realize what I had been holding in for so many years. The revelation was it has truly been hard for me to trust the Father (God) because I never could trust my biological father! Not to say my father was a bad person, or he was not there, but I can honestly say there was no trust in our relationship. My dad was probably the hardest working man I have ever known! He was far from lazy! He would leave for work before the sun would rise and wouldn't return home until the wee hours of the morning, which meant I would be asleep when he left and asleep when he got home.

Sometimes I would be up when he got home and he would be so tired that all he did was take a shower, eat and listen to the game (if there was one on) until he fell asleep.

I know in my heart of hearts I received my work ethic from him. I believe my dad's way of showing love was getting up and going to work every day, which from a man's perspective, is very important. However, if you have children, it is equally important to show and spend time with them. As I got older, I made a lot of mistakes, especially in my late teens and early 20's. I came to realize that some of them were because of the void I felt from not having my dad in my life the way I needed him to be. I can still remember one day talking to my mom about how my dad never taught me certain things I thought a man would want to show his son. Things like how to tie a tie or how to change a tire. My mom said, "But you know what Kevin? Even though he did not show you how you still learned." Even though I did not learn how to tie a tie until I was almost 30, I now sell ties for a living! Go figure! That's how awesome God is! Yes, I didn't learn it when I thought I should have, but not only did I learn it, God made it to where I am now teaching people how to tie them. Romans 8:28 says He makes everything work out for your good!

Manhood can be a tough transition if you don't have the proper foundation for it. People believe manhood begins at 18, but in Jewish Culture it's 13. Young men are thrown a big party to celebrate their move from boyhood to manhood. But if you have not been prepared for the transition, it can be a HUGE STRUGGLE! I look at our society today and everyday young men are going to jail. When you talk to them and ask about their father, most of the time, they say, "I don't know my father." or "I don't have a relationship with my father." You may even hear, "My father is in prison." Which means if the father is in prison or not in the child's life, how can he prepare him for manhood?

In this book, I want to share some important steps of the journey of moving from boyhood to manhood. The Bible says, "When I was a child, I spoke as a child, I understood as a child, I thought as a child, but when I became a man, I put away childish things." (1 Corinthians 13:11) (KJV) The problem with a lot of men today is we are "Toys-R-Us Kids". We don't want to grow up because we like being kids or boys! Being a boy during childhood is good; that's when you are supposed to be a boy. However, when you are the age of a man, you can no longer walk in boy's shoes.

If there is a young man 18 years or older who is reading this book, my hope and prayer is that by the time you get to the last page, your "B-Coming" will have taken flight and propel you to manhood. Once you truly embrace being a man, then manhood will follow. The man I am today did not happen overnight. I bumped my head and made a lot of mistakes. But to God be the glory, I eventually got on the right path and began to walk in my manhood and purpose.

Even though I had a problem with trusting God, I always felt I was destined to do something great in life! I can remember being a boy between the age of 6 and 7 years old. I was traveling with my mom and younger sister, coming from Navasota, Texas on the bus. We arrived at the bus station and were waiting for our luggage. As I was standing there, my eyes became attracted to the automatic doors. The sight of people stepping on the black mat and watching the doors open astonished me! Well, as I was paying attention to the door, I got even closer to watch. I was still in eye distance of my mother, so she felt I was okay because she could still see me. I didn't realize that I had become so close to the door that my arm was now on the glass. As I continued to watch people come and go, someone stepped on the mat and the glass door opened and slid right on my arm! I screamed! My mom must have heard me screaming and hollering and she screamed for help! Workers ran and helped to get the glass door off my arm! They eventually pried my arm loose, and I fell to the ground in serious pain! Not only was I dealing with physical pain, but emotional pain. Can you imagine being a little kid and having an experience like that? People were sure it broke my arm. But as painful as it was, I came away with no broken bones. I didn't even have a bruise! I can remember the pain eventually going away.

Sometimes manhood is a curiosity that draws us to it, but if not handled properly, it can cause you much unnecessary pain. At some point, a man must decide who he is and what he stands for because if he doesn't he will eventually watch life pass him by. Or worse, he will watch the streets chew him up and spit him out! Pain or not, he has to assume the position and accept his responsibility to be a man in every aspect of the word. Especially when it comes to his relationships with others.

If one is going to be willing to go from boyhood to manhood, then boyhood must have something that seems to have fallen by the wayside today and that is RESPECT! Growing up as a young man, my mom taught us to respect those that are older than us. If I was in the presence of my mother and I didn't say "Yes Ma'am", "No Ma'am", "Yes Sir", "No Sir", it would cost me or my eight brothers and sisters a great deal!

My mom may not have had an Ivy League education, but she made sure to instill in us the need to respect those who were older than us; especially our elders. She did not care if they were black, white, green, purple or orange. If you disrespected the elderly, you were in deep trouble. We must teach young men that respecting older people is cool.

The only thing I hate more than a young man being disrespectful to older people is our men being disrespectful. I mean it's one thing for a 14-year-old to have his pants sagging almost all the way to his knees. But to have a 24, 34, or 44 (believe me, it happens) year old man walking around with his pants sagging almost to his knees is downright SAD!!!

I will never forget going to visit my wife's family for the first time in Ville Platte, Louisiana. I saw posted signs everywhere of a young man with his pants sagging. It was a big red line drawn through it and it said, "Pull up your pants or you will get a ticket!" Yep, in that city, it's illegal to walk around with sagging pants! I thought it was one of the best laws that could ever be incorporated. In fact, I would love to see it be a law in so many other cities. A lot of young men do not even know where this comes from! I will not go into detail but at your leisure research (Google) sagging pants. Respect is something that must be earned and not just given. If our young men are going to become the men God has called them to be, they must have respect enough for themselves to pull their pants up!!!

A REAL MAN IS A SPIRITUAL MAN

The day I accepted Christ into my life, He had already been tugging at my heart about making a life change. I can remember one night I was sitting out on my balcony getting high as a kite! I heard the voice literally say, "Okay, enough is enough! If you don't stop doing what you are doing, you will come to see me a lot sooner than planned!" After I heard it I looked at the weed and thought it had me trippin'! But it wasn't the weed! Keep in mind, smoking weed wasn't all I was doing! I was drinking every day! Then drinking made me want to go out and drink even more. I would meet girls and before I knew it, we would be back at my apartment having a great time! But after that night on my balcony, it wasn't the same! Even after that night, if I smoked, drank or went out, I immediately felt out of place.

This went on for a few weeks, so I talked to a friend about what was happening. She asked me if I had ever heard of a Pastor out of Atlanta named Creflo Dollar. I said, "Nope, but he sounds like he is crooked with a name like Dollar." Sorry, I didn't know any better. She told me about his daily teachings on his website. She told me she watched him every morning and that I should check him out. So, I told her I might do it. One day while at work, I decided to see what this Creflo Dollar was all about. I went to his website and looked at one of his programs. Can someone say, "SET UP!" He talked about how God wants you to change your life and He has a great plan for your life. But you must be willing to succumb to your old ways and follow Him! He kept saying it wasn't too late. It wasn't too late. At that moment I jumped up and ran out of my department! Keep in mind I was at work, but I felt like I was in a life or death situation and had to move! I ran out of my department, down the escalators and straight into the chapel (yes, my job had a chapel). I immediately fell on my knees and confessed my sins and asked God to save me!

At the end of my prayer, I asked God to give me a sign it was not too late. Here is where it still blows my mind to this day. There was a lamp hanging from the ceiling. Although I am not 100% sure it wasn't already on when I first ran in the chapel when I asked God to give me a sign that it's not too late, I looked up and the light from the lamp was shining bright! And when I say bright, I mean BRIGHT!!! That day I started on a journey that has totally transformed my life. In the chapters to come, I will share bits and pieces from my journey, in hopes of helping you B come the man that you were designed by God to be.

CHAPTER 1

B Intentional

You were NOT a mistake!

"For I know the plans that I have for you, declares the Lord, „plans for well-being, and not for calamity, in order to give you a future and a hope.
(Jeremiah 29:11) (International Standard Version)

Growing up as a young man, I often battled low self-esteem. I remember thinking my being here was a mistake. I thought maybe that was why my dad and I did not have the relationship I wished we could have had. There were even times when I felt like I wasn't wanted. As a young man, feeling unwanted is the worst feeling in the world! My mom had 5 kids already before me and then I came along as her sixth child. She was only 30 years old. Can you imagine having six kids at 30 years old? I was born in September and she had just turned 30 in June. So because there were five other kids in the house, it could be a challenge trying to give attention to one child. When I was born

I didn't own the position of being the youngest child long. In August of that following year, my sister Sadie was born. I hadn't even turned one yet! Yes, my parents wasted no time! She was born in August and I turned one in September.

B Intentional in redirecting your future to align itself with God's purpose. You've got the power, DO IT!

As I got older, I felt increasingly unwanted. Not so much by my mom, but by my father. I can remember being a young man in high school. I think I was like 14 or 15, playing Junior Varsity basketball in high school. We were playing in a tournament and one of the player's father was watching. After the game, he pulled me to the side and talked with me about some things I needed to change in my game to help me be a better player.

Well the next game, I remembered what he told me and it worked! But then I couldn't help but wonder why my dad couldn't have been there to give me that advice. At the time I couldn't understand that he was working because my friend's dad was a fireman and he still made time to get to his son's game. Like I said before, my dad worked a great deal, so he felt that was his way of showing me love and support. He was making sure the lights stayed on and that we had a roof over my head. As a man, I can honor and respect him for that. But sometimes I needed his presence.

When you have those kinds of issues, the enemy feeds off of them to get you off track. See nothing feels better to a young man than when his dad says, "Good job, son." It does something internally that makes you feel you can take on the world and leap over tall buildings! But when you don't get that, you feel you are worthless and good for nothing. Before you know it, you are getting your gratification from somewhere else like a joint or a bottle. You try to find manhood in sleeping with as many women as you can. But please understand you can't be the man until you meet the Man and invite Him into your life and allow Him to be the Father of all fathers. The Bible says, "I will be a Father to the fatherless." (Psalms 68:5) (King James Version)

However, if you don't know Him, you will think there is nothing in this world for you. I hope and pray that if there is a young man reading this book who may be feeling neglected or unwanted and it seems like your whole life is a mistake; I am here to tell you I have been there and I am telling you that YOU ARE NOT A MISTAKE! You were born with destiny and purpose in mind. It doesn't matter who neglected you or who may have walked out of your life. You still have a purpose! Maybe you grew up with your dad and spent a lot of time with him and you still feel you don't matter. Again, I want to tell you that YOU MATTER! Whenever you have that feeling, turn that pain into power and remember God's words to you in Jeremiah 29:11! Begin to speak it over yourself until you feel better!

You may be a grown man that feel this way. You could be married with children and feel you don't matter or you are worthless. That seed starts at a young age and by the time you are grown it has expanded and is a deeply embedded inside you. But you have to have that same power even as an adult! You have purpose! You still have a destiny! As an adult male you may be struggling with the same low self-esteem as a young man. But you still have the same power to speak positive words over your life and expect positive outcomes. Don't be afraid to B Intentional in redirecting your future to align itself with God's purpose. You've got the power, DO IT!

CHAPTER 2

B Forgiven

I've never been one to shy away from the mistakes I have made in my life. One thing I have learned from the poor decisions I made was that when I were making these decisions I never ever considered anyone else but myself. As a boy you can be selfish. You really only have to think of yourself. As a man, especially a man that is a husband and or a father, there are other people that enter the picture when making decisions. You can never just think of yourself or make choices and decisions for just you. You must always consider those that you are connected to.

The good thing about making bad decisions (if you can say there is a good thing) is the decision you made does not have to be fatal. In the New Testament of the Bible there was a gentleman by the name of Saul who made bad decisions although he loved God he couldn't accept Jesus and all that he stood for so he came against any and everyone who supported Jesus Christ and all that he stood for. Until the day he was on a journey on the road of Damascus when he was knocked off his horse and Jesus began to speak to him. From that moment he was a changed man. What he fought against he began to fight for. He was forgiven and from that forgiveness he was transformed and became probably the second most important person in the New Testament of the Bible. One divine act from God can change your trajectory, it happened for Saul and it can happen for you.

As men you never have to feel like the way you started is the way you have to end. As long as God is breathing life into you, know that you can become someone new. And it's a decision of the mind and the heart. Yes you made the mistakes. Yes you may have hurt others in the process but it doesn't have to end that way, The only way it has to end that way is if you choose to allow it to end that way.

Transformation can begin to take place from the time that you make the decision to push past what was and embrace what will be. Saul was knocked off his horse and was blinded, but he still had to make the decision whether he was going to use this situation for his good. He had a choice, stay the same or to make the necessary transformation.

Forgive yourself today and allow yourself to be transformed completely, B Forgiven!

I say transformation and not change because there is a difference. When you change something you can also change it back to its original state. But when you transform you can never transform back to what you transformed from. A butterfly is not born a butterfly, its transformed into one and once he becomes a butterfly he can never revert back to a caterpillar ever again. That's what happened to Saul who transformed into Paul. He never ever was Saul again!

What type of transformation do you need to make? Maybe it's a struggle for you because of something you have done in your past and maybe you have yet to forgive yourself. Forgive yourself today and allow yourself to be transformed completely, B Forgiven!

CHAPTER 3

B Strong

Be watchful, stand firm in the faith, act like men, be strong. Let all that you do be done in love.
(1 Corinthians 16:13-14) (English Standard Version)

Be strong and courageous. Do not fear or be in dread of them, for it is the Lord your God who goes with you. We will not leave you or forsake you.
(Deuteronomy 31:6) (English Standard Version)

As a man transitions from boyhood into manhood, he must learn to forgive, especially if he wants to be forgiven. Operating in forgiveness takes strength, especially for a man. Before I accepted Christ into my life, my relationship with my dad was a struggle. He just never gave me what I needed to be the man I thought I needed to be.

One day I was riding down the beltway and it was a couple of days before Father's Day. I decided I was going to get my father something. Before, I had never really put any thought into what

I would get him, mainly because I just never had the desire to. One reason was because he never really made a fuss about stuff like that. The other reason was because I didn't know if he deserved anything anyway! I may have made a Father's Day card or something, but never really put any thought into a gift once I became an adult. But on that day in 2009, I had my mind made up that I was going to get him something. By this time I had made some changes in my life and I wasn't living the kind of life that I had been living in the past. God had really done a number on my heart and the anger I once had for my father had turned into love! I had also made up my mind that I was going to buy him a gift and spend a little time with him.

My dad had taken sick the last few years of his life and was in and out of the hospital. Just a few years prior my dad had fallen and broken his hip. He had to have emergency surgery that didn't go so well and became even more ill. It was touch and go for a minute. I can remember going to the hospital but it wasn't to see him. It was really to make sure my mom was okay. It really didn't bother me that he was in the hospital not doing well. All I could think about was the well being of my mom! The wall of hurt was high for me and even my dad's sickness couldn't bring it down. In fact, the only thing that could was when I truly allowed Christ in my heart and He tore it down.

In the days leading up to that Father's Day, I stopped and grabbed him a shirt. Not just any shirt. I mean I really took my time and picked out a real nice shirt and took it to him on Father's Day. We sat up and watched a baseball game on television and listened to the radio. Yep, my dad loved listening to the game on the radio because that's how he had grown up listening to it. We sat and talked and laughed for a while until he got sleepy. He was telling me he had a doctor's appointment the next day and I asked him if he wanted me to help him take a bath before I left. God had really done a number on my heart! But he declined. He was the type that wanted to lay down once he got tired. So I helped him get in the bed and told him I was about to leave. But before I left I said, "Daddy, I love you!" His words were, "Okay, yeah I love y'all too." I said to myself, "But I am the only one here…"

I didn't understand what that meant but a month later, I fully understood. My dad went to the doctor the very next day in the shirt I had bought for him for Father's Day. Unfortunately, his health wasn't good, so they sent him from the doctor's office to the hospital. He had congestive heart failure and his heart was getting weak. It was making him so tired that all he wanted to do was rest. When I got to the hospital, I just sat there and talked to him. Every day I would go see him and spend as much time with him as I could. Then one day as I was getting ready to leave the hospital, I said, "Daddy, I love you!" His exact words, right before he fell asleep were, "I love you too!" Man, I cried all the way down the hallway to the elevator. I had never heard him say those words to me (at least not at an age I could remember). It meant EVERY-

THING to me! It became clear to me that God wouldn't let my dad die the first time he was in the hospital or any of the other times because he hadn't told me he loved me yet.

No child should grow up without hearing their father tell them they love them! If you are reading this book now and you have a son that you can talk to, call and tell him that you love him! Put this book down now and go and let him know! Please don't think it doesn't matter because I am a witness that it does!

To a son that is reading this book, if your father is still living and you are able to tell him you love him, GO NOW! Don't wait! Do it now! You may have to do like I did and initiate the "I love you" first! I realized that the first time when he expressed his love for us "all" was because he probably had not told any of us (myself, my brothers and my sisters) that he loved us.

July 18, 2009, I saw my dad take his last breath here on earth and to be honest, I was at peace. My dad had lived a long and hard working life. He was very independent and preferred to do things his own way. Plus, he told my mom that he never wanted to be hooked up to machines and life support again. He told her to pull the plug if his health ever got bad enough. Spoken like only he could speak. But by the time he passed away, the love that he gave was not what I perceived that I needed, but it was the best he had to offer! As I grew with God, I realized that my earthly father's love was worth being thankful for!

A man will need to be strong enough to face his demons and conquer them. For me it was a perceived rejection by my father, for you it may be abandonment, abuse, or neglect. B Strong, with God all things are possible.

There are days in my life when no matter how old I get, I will remember. I probably won't remember everything about them, but for the most part, I will remember enough to relive the day I lost my mom. November 13, 2015, was probably the saddest day of my life. My mom had been in and out of the hospital, dealing with health issues. For two years she had beat the odds once but on this visit she just wasn't doing well. I was a mama's boy and she was my best friend in addition to being my mother. Talk about needing the strength of God, I really needed Him that day.

My mom was in a skilled nursing facility getting the care she so desperately needed and the ambulance would come get her from the facility and take her to get her dialysis. She suffered from renal failure as well as congestive heart failure. When she arrived at the dialysis center, her nurse noticed how low her blood pressure had fallen so she immediately asked the ambulance to take her to the ER. Not only was her blood pressure low, but when she arrived at the hospital, she was not her normal self. Everyone knew my mom was never at a loss for words and she always said what came to mind. She didn't mean any harm; that was just JB (Mama)! So she got to the ER and they quickly admitted her. My sister got the call that she was there and immediately called me. I got there as soon as I could.

Because she was not at her normal healthcare hospital, I asked for her to be transferred there. I wanted her to be where her doctors and nurses knew her and had a relationship with her. I wanted her to be where I worked. That way I could make sure that she was properly taken care of. Not to say the other hospital couldn't, I just felt better with her being there. All throughout the day my mom slept. She didn't want to eat or talk or watch tv. All she did was sleep. Even in her sleep, she looked like she was in so much pain. I can't describe in words how it made me feel seeing the lady that took care of me so many times when I was sick laying there in pain and I couldn't do anything! The only time my mom got up was when she heard me playing Al Green (one of her favorite singers). She popped up for a second and eventually laid back down.

Before long, the transfer was accepted and the nurse had me sign the necessary paperwork and was getting ready to call the ambulance to transfer us. She walked out and I told mom that we were getting ready to go to her usual hospital. She frowned, shook her head and said, "No, no no!" Not even 10 minutes later the Charge Nurse ran in and said her blood pressure and heart rate had dropped at an alarming rate. I didn't know that they had been watching her heart rate since her arrival. The nurse began to call her name in a very loud voice to get her attention. By this time, other nurses ran in! Mama was not responding! So I jumped up

---

B Strong and allow the lover of your soul to have full control of your life even in the most devastating times, He is our strength!

---

and yelled, "MAMA!" She opened her eyes for a split second and then closed them back. Then the nurse asked the charge nurse if he wanted to call a Code. Because I work at a hospital, I knew what that meant! They did and asked me to step out. The doctor from the code team walked up to me and told me what was happening and asked how far they should go in the code. I immediately said, "Sir, do whatever you have to do to save my mother!"

While they were pumping my mother's chest, I was on the phone with all of my mother's sisters, asking them to get to the hospital as fast as they could! I didn't want to tell them what was going on because I didn't want them to get into an accident on the way to the hospital. They worked on her for an hour! Pumping and pumping and pumping. But my mom had tired out and I eventually just asked them to stop because she had had enough! At 8:06, November 13, my mom had passed away. You talk about being devastated! The hardest part for me was when my sisters and brothers began to arrive to the hospital. I had to tell them, one by one, what happened and that mom had passed. I wrestled and struggled with the huge decision that I had made that day. Did I make a mistake by telling her that we were about to go to another hospital? I asked myself that because it wasn't even 10 minutes after I told her that she coded! If I wouldn't have told her, would she still be here with us? With me being the only sibling there at the time, I didn't get any suggestions from them. I didn't know if they were upset because I told her. I had so many different thoughts going through my head.

But that's just how the enemy does things. He tries to make everything that happens in your life worse than it really is. My mom had passed and that hurt like hell! Please excuse the language, but if you had the same kind of relationship with your mom as I did with mine, you understand. The enemy wanted to turn my grief into torment! He had me thinking it was all my fault. Why in the world did you tell her? You know if you hadn't said anything, she would still be here. You talk too much! All these things were going through my head as I was trying to be one of the siblings to make the final preparation for my mom's funeral. We had just done this for my father 6 years earlier and here we were again!

Coming up I was taught that you are always held responsible for the choices you make in life. It's up to you whether the choices you make are right or wrong and it may take some time before you are able to tell if it was a good or bad choice. Then sometimes it doesn't even take long. You know the moment you make the decision whether it's good or bad. Remember, regardless of the outcome, God is always there with you to bring strength to your weak places. He becomes our strength when we invite Him into our situation. Sometimes being strong is acknowledging the fact that you aren't and allowing Him to be your present help in a time of trouble and disappointment. B Strong and allow the lover of your soul to have full control of your life even in the most devastating times, He is our strength!

CHAPTER 4

B You

There are times I remember not really liking who I was as a person. Although the Bible says we are made in God's image, I looked at myself and didn't like what I saw. When you don't like the person you are, it is easy to try and be someone else and that can be dangerous! You have to know that God created you just the way He wanted you to be. I once had the pleasure of reading a book called Identity Crisis by Author DeMonica Gladney. It talked about having an identity crisis and how to not let anyone steal your identity. I remember reading it one day on a flight to Los Angeles and I could not put it down. It was shedding light on how the enemy comes to try to rob you of your identity. See the enemy starts at an early age by trying to tell you what

> B You, there's no one else who can do YOU like you! God designed it that way!

you are not or what you can't and won't be. He even tries to tell you that you were a mistake and nobody cares about you! I know because he used to try to tell me the same things! It wasn't until I became closer to my heavenly Father that my true self-identity began to come forth. I learned that being me was the best person for me to be. I was watching Steve Harvey one day (I have always been a huge fan). Everything he does makes me believe Steve is the Man! Although I have yet to meet him, I do believe that one day Mr. Harvey and I are going to meet and get to know each other.

One day while watching his show, I found myself saying, "I WANT TO BE THE NEXT STEVE HARVEY!" I mean, everything he does amazes me! From his positive words, his relationships with people, the way he is always as clean as a whistle from head to toe! However, I remember just as fast as I said it, I was rebuked by the Holy Spirit! He said, "Instead of wanting to be the next Steve Harvey, why don't you just focus on being the first Kevin D. Boudreaux!" He said it loud too! What was amazing was as soon as the spirit said it, I said to myself, "YES! That's a great idea! Be the best ME I can be! The ME God created! The world already has a Steve Harvey. What this world needs now is a Kevin D. Boudreaux. No one can fit that but me! So from that day, I embraced me. Not only that but I truly enjoy it! Even as I write this, I am smiling and happy about being me!

You will soon learn that when you accept you and be cool with being you, then that shows God appreciation for Him creating you! Please don't misunderstand me, there is nothing wrong with having people you admire or heroes as some may call them. There are people who may inspire you to pattern your life like theirs. But you should never want to be someone else more than you want to be yourself, especially as a man. If there is something you don't like about yourself, you have the power to change it. I dealt with weight issues. At one point I was weighing 280+lbs! I couldn't stand it! But as much as people would encourage me or tell me that I could lose the weight, it wasn't until I made up my mind that I could make the change that I actually began to make the change! When you are cool with being you and you don't like something about you, you have a great power on the inside of you (the Holy Spirit) to change it. B You, there's no one else who can do YOU like you! God designed it that way!

CHAPTER 5

B Free

Have you ever walked through life like you were bound and it seems as though you just don't have the freedom you want and desire? It's like that old saying, "I take two steps forward and get pushed back three!" In the Bible John 8:36 says, "Whom the Son sets free is free indeed." So if you know that Jesus has set you free over 2000 years ago (when He died on the cross) through the shedding of His blood, you are set free! Yes, when He gave up his life, the shackles on and over your life were released! So when you are feeling bound you have to remember that YOU ARE FREE! Let Freedom Ring!

When I was a young man, my mom would be reluctant to let my sister and I go outside and play freely because of the neighborhood I grew up in. Drugs and violence ran wild so we didn't have the freedom to roam around like we wanted to. But every year we would take a trip to Huntsville, Texas to visit family. Although it was less than 100 miles away, it felt like we were going to Disney Land! To me, the best part was the freedom we would have running around the country. There was so much land and we would get with our cousins and have fun, fun, fun! If we didn't go to the country, we would be out at my great uncle's house. Now he lived in what they called "town." But their town was not like our town. It was still a lot safer than our neighborhood. We had just as much freedom at his house as we did out in the country at Madear's (my grandmother) house. We didn't have to worry about the drugs, violence or gangs in Huntsville because those types of things just didn't take place out there. At least not in the areas we visited. There is nothing like freedom! Unfortunately, we don't appreciate freedom until it is taken from us!

I remember one Sunday morning after a night of partying and drinking. I brought a club friend of mine home with me. I call her a club friend because honestly, that's the only time we talked or hung out. So this particular morning I was on the way to take her home. I was so hung over and sleepy. In the back of my mind, I was thinking about how I really wanted to hurry and get her home so that I could go back home and get back in the bed. I dropped her off and jetted as fast as I could. Halfway back home I got pulled over for speeding! I am thinking to myself, "Oh no! This is not going to be good!" My initial thought was that he would smell alcohol on my breath from last night and would want me to take a breathalyzer test or something. He explained to me that when he pulled my information up, I had warrants for my arrest for outstanding tickets! He said he was going to have to place me under arrest! WHAT? Yep, I was known for not paying my traffic tickets.

Even if I went to court, I didn't pay the tickets and it had finally caught up with me! He told me that if I could get someone To pay the tickets once we got down to the jail house, I would be able to be released. Once we got down there, so that's what I did and it seemed to take forever! No windows to look out of. I couldn't go as I pleased because I didn't do what I was supposed to do. My freedom had been snatched away from me and I did NOT like it at all! Then to make matters worse, once the tickets were paid in that city, I was still not released because I had outstanding tickets in another city! Which meant those tickets had to be paid before I could be released!

That's kind of what the enemy does! You think you are about to be released in an area, only to realize you are still tied up in another area! What felt like days, only took a few hours. But just the fact that my freedom was taken away from me shook me. I didn't like it and never wanted to experience that again! Not to mention it cost me more than it would have cost me to have paid the tickets the first time around. Plus, the cost to get my car out of the pound! I don't see how people can go to jail or prison and get out and desire to go back. Perhaps they feel that the system brings them a "no worries" freedom. That's just crazy to me! People telling you what to do, when to do it, how to do it and how fast it has to be done!

That is why having mental freedom is just as important as any other freedom. One of the best ways to have mental freedom is to make sure you renew you mind every day. The Bible says, "And be not conformed to this world; but be ye transformed by the renewing of your mind, that ye may prove what is that good, and acceptable, and perfect, will of God." (Romans 12:2) (KJV) If you want mental freedom you have to renew your mind. I can't say that enough! If you want to walk in manhood, you can't allow your mind to think like a little boy.

Case and point, me not taking care of those speeding tickets was a young boy's thought, not a grown man's! A grown man would have taken care of what needed to be taken care of because he would realize that there would be consequences if he didn't, and that they would cost him a lot more later on. True manhood understands that having to spend the extra money later could cause him to have to take finances out of his home for his family. As a man, that wouldn't sit well with him. And if it did, he would not be walking in manhood. As a man with a family, you always want to make sure you do what's best for them. They are your main priority. In a man's life, it should be God, your wife and kids, and then everything else. I will not say that this principle is a principle that I took to immediately. It took some time to learn this, but I was so glad that I finally did. Now I look forward to helping other young men achieve and excel in this area.

I try my best to lead by example. I try to stop young men from making some of the same mistakes I made. A lot of young men that I am close to ask me about my past. I am honest with them, not so that I can feel like a player or like I had it going on, but more so to try and show them that the way I went is not the way to travel! I try not to make it look glamorous or exciting and

B Free to be the man God called you to be!

fun. Although during those times it seemed like we were having a great time and did not really care about what was to follow. But there were times that I would wake up from a night of partying and clubbing and not remember what happened the night before. It sounds like fun but to be honest, that's sad and very, very scary! There are so many things that could have happened to me back in those days! I thank God that social media was not out or hadn't blown up like it is today! With the way I was, I know without a shadow of a doubt that I would have been all over social media and not in a good way! But thank God for His grace! He kept me covered even when I didn't realize it or didn't even care! Nobody can tell me that there is no such thing as God's grace because I know it covered me! That is why I try to tell young men whenever I get a chance that I was able to go through and did what I did so that they don't have to. I know sometimes they may not understand it all, but if they would just keep living and growing they will soon learn and see what I am talking about.

The desire of wanting to be accepted and be in the in crowd is so big now. I mean it was big when I was coming up, but it's even bigger now. Either you are one of the cool and popular people or you are just a dud or a nobody; a nerd! At 11 or 12, that is the last thing you want to be considered. Unfortunately, some people never grow out of it. When I was in elementary school, I was part of a group of boys that was called the *5th Ward Posse*! Yep, we felt like we were the gang of the school and if you had a problem with one of us, you had a problem with all of us! We had it set so that students, teachers and principals thought we were a gang who did and sold drugs. So much so that one day we were called down to the office one by one and interviewed. They asked us if we had drugs on campus. We all told them we didn't but they didn't believe us. So they stripped searched us all to check and see. Seems as though someone had tipped them off that we had drugs and guns at school. But come to find out we didn't have anything. However, because of the way we carried ourselves, we became targets. That is why I try to tell young men to try not to carry themselves in a way that will bring negative attention their way.

Trust me, especially in my early 20's, I made a lot of bad choices. From drinking and driving to taking my rent money and going to party with it, then looking crazy when it was time to pay rent! I can also remember the time when a group of friends had gone out partying and on the way home, I was so intoxicated that when I got behind the wheel, I was swerving all over the place. Before I knew it, the lights began flashing behind me! Yep, I had gotten pulled over and it wasn't pretty. Thank God the cop didn't want to take me to jail. He told me he couldn't let me drive home but if I had money for a tow truck, he would let me get my truck towed and I wouldn't go to jail. I was so glad that I had enough cash to do so. The tow truck towed my vehicle to my mom's house which happened to be the closest to where I got pulled over and would have been cheaper to get towed there instead of on the other side of town where I lived at the time. My mom came outside because she saw the lights shining from the tow truck. She just looked at me and shook her head. She said, "Kevin, I didn't raise you like this!" I just said, "Mama, I know." As if getting behind the wheel the first time after drinking wasn't a bad enough choice, after the tow truck left, I jumped in my vehicle and went on about my business! I had a girl I was trying to get to and couldn't miss out. Talk about bad choices! Now what if I would have hit and killed someone? Can you imagine how terrible that would've been? Or worse, how would the officer have felt if the guy he had just had mercy on, got back in his car and killed someone? Thank God that His grace was on me and protected me even when I didn't realize it! That's enough to give God praise!

I would like to think that the older a man gets, the better choices he makes. But sadly, that's not the truth. If a man wants to walk in true manhood, he has to be willing to make better and proper choices, especially when it comes to his family. A man should always put his family's needs ahead of his own. I can't stand to see a man looking out for himself and his family is in desperate need of something. Even more so towards your kids. No child asks to come into this world and since you had a lot to do with it, you need to take care of your responsibilities. You owe it to them to raise them and be the best father you can be. Even if you and the mother may not have been able to make things work with each other.

The Bible says, "Choose ye this day, whom you shall serve." (Joshua 24:15) (KJV) Even when it comes to serving and loving God, it's a choice. God doesn't make you choose, He just holds you accountable for the choices you make. A key to making a good choice, or a manhood choice, is understanding that the choice you make not only affects you, but it will affect someone else in a positive way. Like my choosing to write this book not only affects me, but prayerfully it will positively affect anyone that reads it. My prayer is that a man would read this and make the choice to be better than he was before he picked the book up. My intention is not to poke at or talk down to anyone. I just want to let men know that the time is now to take a positive step forward into manhood and walk in the fullness thereof. We are natural born leaders and leaders lead from the bottom and not from the top. Our shoulders are built to have our families stand on them. It took me a long time to learn this principle, but I am standing as a witness of the fact that when you take care of your family, God will take care of you even the more. God loves to see a man taking care of his family as a leader. But just like God loves to see it, the enemy hates it! But the only thing he can do is get you to quit, to think about yourself only and let others fend for themselves.

I can remember when my family and I were going through a terrible transition and it was causing silent frustration and problems in our home. As the head of the household, I knew I had to do something; not just for me, but for my entire family! It was real bad. For a husband to look at his wife and know that she is looking to him for answers is extremely difficult. But I knew I had to go to God for guidance and direction before making any moves. Men, you want to seek God's counsel before making a huge decision concerning your family. "Trust in the Lord with all thine heart; and lean not unto thine own understanding. In all thy ways acknowledge him, and he shall direct your paths." (Proverbs 3:5-6) (KJV) I don't consider myself to be a Bible scholar but there are some scriptures that you just know! So that's what I did. After I prayed, I asked God to give me a chance. It wasn't 15 minutes later that the chance came. As a husband, a father and as a man, I did what I had to do! My wife was standing there and witnessed it all! Husbands, you can probably agree, there is nothing like you allowing the male lion roar to rise up inside of you and your lioness is right there, witnessing it firsthand!

RRRROOOOAAAARRRR!!! Sometimes that's what a man has to do! On that day, I did it! I never looked back, nor did I regret doing what I did. All because I knew that what I was doing wasn't just for me, but it was for those whom God had given me to oversee.

There are plenty of times in the past when my house would be quiet; everyone would be asleep and I would be praying and talking to God! Boys run, men stand! B Free to be the man God called you to be!

CHAPTER 6

B Consistent

Real manhood requires consistency. We can't be fair weather men, especially in our marriages and parenting. When my middle daughter, Ke'Bria (yes, she's named after me), was born, her mom and I tried to make things work for a while. But because of the way I was partying and hanging out and doing everything except spending time with my family, I wasn't trying to be the family man they needed me to be. Ke'Bria's mother took all she could take and eventually told me it was time to move on and move out! Yes, if I wasn't going to be what they wanted and needed me to be, it was time for me to make a move. In all honesty, I couldn't blame her. All she wanted was a family and a man that wanted a family. So did I. However, it just wasn't me at the time. When I decided I was ready, she was long gone.

The bad part about it was that I still had a daughter to raise. She was a little over 1 and although her mom and I weren't able to make things work, my daughter was still my responsibility. Fathers listen, before I continue, let me put this plug in. MEN, IF YOU HAVE KIDS, PLEASE, PLEASE, PLEASE TAKE CARE

OF YOUR KIDS! They did not ask to come here. You laid down and made them. It's your responsibility to take care of them on a regular basis! I say that because after Ke'Bria's mom and I went our separate ways, my duties as a father were lacking. I was very inconsistent on doing my part. If it was my turn to take Ke'Bria to school and I went out the night before, 9 times out of 10, I would over sleep the next morning. That meant my daughter would be late to school. I did this repeatedly because I wanted to go out and have a good time with a bunch of strangers instead of being in a position to take my daughter (who was depending on me) to school. I became more and more inconsistent, even down to not picking her up on the weekends like I was supposed to. If I had a party or a date or both, they took priority over me spending time with my child. I don't write this to boast or brag, but to bring light to the situation and to tell men who are doing this to stop and stop now! I had gotten so bad that when I did go get her, sometimes she didn't even recognize me and would cry when we would leave.

One morning I went to pick her up for school. I knocked on the door and I could hear her running to the door screaming with joy. Unfortunately, she was screaming a name that wasn't mine! It wasn't Daddy or Kevin. She was shouting for her mom's current boyfriend. Once her mom opened the door and Ke'Bria saw it was me, she had this disappointed look on her face. Man I was crushed! I had lost the respect and love of my daughter and now she was afraid of me because she didn't know me well enough to go with me. She finally got in the car and as we were riding down the street I looked through my rearview mirror and I could see tears coming down her face. I could have literally been bought for a penny that day! Who could I blame? Certainly not my daughter nor her mom. I couldn't even blame her boyfriend because he was only stepping up and doing what I wasn't doing. I couldn't be mad at anyone but the man in the mirror, ME! And that day I made the decision on the HOV lane on I-45 South; heading downtown, that I was going to do and be better. And from that day on, I have been. Am I perfect? No, not by a long shot! But I can say that from that time to now, I have been consistent. I never tried to aim for perfection but for consistency. If I can remain consistent, that would be just as good as perfect in my book. Men, don't strive for perfection, strive for consistency. I realized I was doing the exact same thing to my daughter that my dad had done to me. I was neglecting her and her needs. It is really easy to repeat a cycle that has taken place in your childhood. I made up my mind that the cycle would stop with me and I immediately began to clean up my act and slowly but surely, I did! It's a great feeling when you can look at yourself in the mirror and be happy with the man you are becoming!

Sometimes walking in manhood may not be easy, but it's necessary. When I look at today's society and what is taking place in our nation, I have to ask myself if all of this would go on if we had men doing more of what we were created to do. Men, you have to be able to tap into your full potential and know that you know that you know that God created you for a purpose, with purpose, to fulfill purpose! The enemy is only doing his job as a coon and a snake in the grass to get you to walk away from your purpose! Understand the enemy cannot stop you physically, but if he could get in your head and mind and get you to forfeit what God has called you to do, then he has won! He is like one of those friends that try to get you to skip school as a child and tries to convince you that he does it all the time. "It's not that bad and you won't get caught," so he says. He sells it so well that you finally give in and skip school like he suggested, only for you to get caught and get in trouble. When this happens, he is nowhere to be found! You get in trouble and take the fall, all the while he is somewhere on the sidelines laughing!

B Consistent in your spiritual walk by mimicking Christ Jesus, particularly in your relationships and the fruits of that consistency will not only bless you, but everyone around you!

As men, we have to be more like the biblical Job! He was a man that God could trust! Remember, in the book of Job, God recommended him to the enemy, already knowing that he would be able to withstand whatever he threw his way. Job went through a lot and lost a lot, but even in the toughest of times, Job stood! Because of his stand, he not only got everything that he lost back, but he got back DOUBLE! All because he kept standing! That's what we as men need to do today! Keep standing! Stand for our families, stand for our neighborhoods and stand for our churches! If we can stand for those things that God has called us to stand for, surely He will give us the strength to stand and be with us while we stand. His word says, "… If God be for us, who can be against us?" (Romans 8:31) (KJV) Don't get me wrong, standing as a man is not easy.

Men go through different types of adversities every day. Challenges that range from providing for our families to dealing with issues at work and world crisis. One of the biggest problem is when we are young men or boys and people want to rush us to be men. They don't take the time to show us what a man is supposed to be. I think one of the biggest issues is when you tell a boy to be a man; you rob him of his childhood experience!

I believe every young man should be able to go ride his bike or play football after school or sit up on Saturday mornings and watch wrestling while eating a bowl of Frosted Flakes! Wow, I just had a flashback! But as a young boy, I loved doing those things whenever possible! I especially loved riding my bike. I did it but didn't do it a lot because of the neighborhood we lived in. When I did, I absolutely loved it! My only problem was that whenever I did get a chance to, my younger sister just had to go along with me. I preferred to roll alone but my mom would say if she couldn't go, then I couldn't go! So off we went, and it wasn't just riding my bike either. Man, if I was going to the Rec (the place where I played and learned how to play basketball), she went with me. As she got older, she fell in love with basketball and after a while; she didn't want to just go; she wanted to play! You know how hard that was to have your little sister rolling with you, wanting to play basketball with a bunch of dudes? Most of my friends were flirts and hot young boys, so I had to watch the boys in the game and watch her too in order to make sure he wasn't trying to grab or hold my sister too close. I hated that! I think she knew it too, but just like I did, she loved the game and she became good at it! She played all four years in high school, just like me.

Every young man needs to have that experience growing up. I feel so sorry for those young men whose dads are not at home and their moms have to tell them that they are the man of the house because their dad is not around. She has just taken away their boyhood experience. But at the same time, that boyhood experience NEEDS to have an expiration date! Sooner and not later, your boyhood should move into manhood! The only thing worse than a young boy trying to be a man is a man trying to be a young boy! For the life of me, I cannot understand how a 30-year-old man can sit at home, playing a video game all day and would allow his hard working wife to come home from work and ask her what she is cooking! The craziest part is the wife asking him what he wants to eat! Look, the Bible says, "… If any would not work, neither should he eat." (2 Thessalonians 3:10) (KJV) Ladies, please do not be one of those women who accept a man not doing anything for himself or for you but thinks he can be a man around the house or call shots! No, the only shot he needs to be calling is a job shot! Don't be found guilty of giving a man full benefits while he is still walking in his boyhood shoes!

July 3, 2010, was the day God blessed me to be a husband. Man, that day was a day I will never forget. My future wife created a wedding that we could both look back on and be proud of. So many people were happy and excited for us, but unfortunately, a lot of people weren't. We chose not to focus on those that weren't and focused on those that were. The entire week leading up to our big day, it rained! As a matter of fact, we had to move our rehearsal dinner from one location to another because of the rain.

The original location had an electrical problem. I was a nervous wreck because we had to find another place that wouldn't go over a budget that was growing extremely thin. I didn't want to worry my wife about it because she already had enough on her plate concerning the wedding. Thank goodness the church we were having our rehearsal dinner had a reception hall for a great price! Even with that price, I still didn't have it. My oldest brother (and best man), who always seems to have my back, took care of everything. I never told him about the situation, he just took care of it and told me to go to the rehearsal. I was so grateful!

God knows how to send an angel to take care of your needs like only He can. The dinner went great. My mom, sisters, and sister-in-law prepared the food, decorations and made sure we all had a great time! I was finally able to relax after a long hard day. The weather was so bad that day that I didn't even think my mom and I were going to make it to the rehearsal. Her neighborhood had flooded, and we were stuck! Mom could see the worry and frustration on my face and she came up to me like only a mom could and told me everything was going to be okay. She said we would get there just fine. We did just that!

Growing up, there were times when I started thinking I was grown and my mom and I didn't see eye to eye on a lot of things. But it never ever failed that she would be there when I needed a special piece of love that only she could provide. She always made sure I had it. It rained like cats and dogs on the wedding day! Because of the rain, our wedding was almost 2 hours late getting started. Again, mom couldn't get to the church because it was flooding in her neighborhood. A lot of others were having problems getting to the church as well. Eventually we got started and had an amazing wedding! I cried, my wife cried, friends cried! It was just a beautiful day! And we praised God! Afterward, our reception was just as nice. That was over 8 years ago and to this day, my wife and I still have people telling us what a beautiful wedding it was.

It was a very humbling experience. I never try to be big headed or boast about anything. I try my best to always stay grateful and thankful for all God has done for me. He has truly made a way out of no way numerous times in my life. Even in my marriage, I know without a doubt that God's hand is and will always be in it. I will tell any man that may be wanting or preparing to get married to make sure he seeks God first. Not just that but wait for His response. He will begin to send wise counsel your way who will help you prepare for a life changing move like marriage. One thing is for sure, if you want to be and are thinking about marriage and you want your marriage to be successful, you cannot be selfish! I will say that again. A man cannot be selfish! I believe that when a marriage begins to fall apart; the man is or has gotten selfish. Whether it be he works too much and doesn't spend time with his family or he has decided that he wants to have an extramarital affair. It mostly boils down to the man taking a selfish role and allowing his wants and fleshly desires to take control of a covenant that he made before God!

This is why marriage counseling is so important. Whether it be from your Pastor or an older man who is or has been married before. It shouldn't be from someone who's going to give you some type of male chauvinistic garbage. It should be someone who has been where you are trying to go and can give you the advice you need and not so much the advice you want. Trust me, you are going to need it! It won't be long after you say I do and the honeymoon has come and gone that you are wondering what you have gotten yourself into! Men listen, marriage is a very important thing, and it is extremely important to God. God considers a marriage between a husband and his wife to be likened unto that of His marriage to the church! That's why I keep saying you can't be selfish.

We can't get so pumped up about the honeymoon and all the fun that comes with it. Trust me, it's supposed to be all of that, but you have to make sure you have made the proper preparation. I wish I would have prepared a little better myself for my marriage. Men, don't try to focus on preparing your wife for marriage! Use this time to prepare yourself and keep your wife lifted in prayer. Ask God to prepare her. In the past, I have seen so many men try to tell their fiancée what to do in order to be prepared for their marriage. Things like making sure she knows how to cook certain meals or how to take care of the house. But understand that the lady you are about to make your helpmate is not your mother! She is your wife! They are two totally different people! We have to be able to bear the majority of the weight in the marriage and in the household. We are the foundation. Everything is built on us. The great part is that God doesn't expect us to bear this alone. He wants to help us. He wants us to cast all of our cares and needs upon Him so that He can give us the help we need. In turn, we can be the help that our family needs. I truly believe that if any man wants and desires to be a good husband, he has to have a personal relationship with God. He has to be your guide. He has to be your compass. He has to be your Leader!

If you are reading this and you don't have a relationship with God as your Father, I would like to invite you to make Him the head of your life right now! You may be saying, "Kevin, are you serious? You are trying to bring me to Christ through this book?" My answer is YES!

It's as simple as you saying, "Lord Jesus, I know You are real! I know you created me and You sent Your Son Jesus to die on the cross for my sins! I repent of my sins now and I ask You to come into my life!" Congratulations! You have just accepted Christ into your life! Welcome to the family! Men, don't just do this for marriage, do it for yourself! As a matter of fact, I would recommend that you develop a good, stable relationship with God before you even consider marriage. That way you can ask Him to show you and lead you to the woman He wants you to marry. It could be someone that you were expecting, but a lot of times it's someone you were not! Either way, if God leads you to it, He has a plan for it!

I think a man should not only be spiritually prepared for marriage but also financially and emotionally. Make sure you have a home and a job so that you will be able to provide and meet the needs of your wife! Don't marry a woman thinking or expecting her to take care of you! Even if she makes more money than you, it is still your job to lead! Make sure you have gotten all of your partying, staying out late, and hanging out with the guys six nights a week out of your system. You are taking on a wife, so your priorities change as well as your responsibilities. That doesn't mean you can't have a guys' night out every so often (because you will need it), but you can't do it the same way you did as a single man. Once you have kids, it's almost impossible! Make sure you have done the groundwork before you get married. You have to understand that it's no more just you, but now it's you and her. And the two shall become one.

After marriage, it was no longer she and I. It became us! We are a team and in everything we do; we have to have each other in mind. We have to have each other's backs. We are not just husband and wife; we are friends! Don't get so lost in trying to be your wife's husband that you neglect the fact that you need to be her friend as well. You have to be able to be goofy and play around with her. Life can't be all serious all the time. It's tough enough being married. I think when you are friends, it just helps the relationship even more. Some of you may think all husbands and wives are friends automatically. Unfortunately, that is not always the case. Some husbands and wives don't even like each other! They are just together because of family, kids or financial reasons. Can you imagine being tied to someone that you don't even like? That makes for a frustrating marriage! So make sure you are friends with your wife.

B Consistent in your spiritual walk by mimicking Christ Jesus, particularly in your relationships and the fruits of that consistency will not only bless you, but everyone around you!

CHAPTER 7

B Disciplined

Sometimes discipline can be very tough for men who may not be used to it. A young man that has spent time in the armed forces compared to a man that has not may make being disciplined a lot harder. In the service, you go through something called Basic Training. It helps you learn discipline. People who have been a part of the armed forces are known for being well disciplined individuals. It takes focus and dedication.

Have you ever tried to discipline your kids? It takes careful and precise teaching. Do not do like my dad! He had to administer discipline once, and I do mean once! That's all it took for me. I was about 5 or 6 years old. My mom and I were watching TV and my dad was getting ready to go out. My mom asked him to go get me some chicken before he went out. He said no! I guess the answer he gave my mom was not to my liking, so I said, "Man, go get the ---- chicken!" Yes, I did! Not sure where I learned that word from, but I must have wanted my dad to bring us the chicken more than my mom did because I just blurted out the words before I knew it. But after I said what I said, it was time for me to face the consequences! I can still see the picture over 30 years later!

My dad was walking out the door and once he heard me say what I said, he stopped in the middle of the door, put his beer down and came towards me while taking his belt off! I immediately jumped behind my mom but there was nothing she could do! I called myself being a man and did what any man would do. I faced the repercussion of what I had done. Man, that whooping I received is permanently imprinted on my mind! Now you know that I have gotten a ton of whoopings growing up, but the majority of them came from my mother. My dad only whooped me that once! After that, I never tried to get a whooping from him again!

That's what happens when we try to get our young men to be grown men too fast. They face the consequences of a grown man! It hurts my heart to see a teenager or young man getting in trouble for stealing or a crime that you would think they were too young to be doing. They know their name is in the system and everyone knows that once that happens it's hard to get out. Let's say you commit a crime at the age of 12 and you are convicted for it. That incident can follow you for the rest of your life. Even if you turn your life around and decide to walk the straight and narrow path that incident will still follow you. When you try to get into college that incident will come up. When applying for a job, they ask if you have ever been convicted of a felony. They will see you have something in your records and that just doesn't look

> **B Disciplined because you may become the standard for those boys and men around you. Your life will be the better for it!**

good on your application. It could very well damage your chances of getting a job. Some places won't hire a person with past felonies on their record.

That's why when it comes to raising our young men, we have to make sure we are showing and not just telling them what they need to do as young men. Even if a man has made it to manhood and did not have a man in his life growing up, they need to be mentored. I don't have a son of my own to raise and for a while; I felt bad about that. I just felt that every man should have a son. But I now understand that was not God's plan for my life. Instead of me having a son or sons, His plan was for me to empower a Nation of young men. Maybe if I would have had a son of my own, I would have only been able to focus on just him or them. But with me not having a son, it frees me up to give my time and attention to a group of young men. You just never know what God has planned for your life. I have a nice group of nephews, 10 to be exact. All of them are special to me. I was so glad that as they became older; I made some major changes in my life that allowed me to be someone they could look up to and not someone they developed bad habits from! I remember staying with one of my oldest nephews, Devion, because his parents worked crazy hours. I used to get up and get him dressed and catch the bus with him to go meet his dad. I literally saw him grow up and graduate from high school. He then got accepted into and attended Baylor University! Baylor wasn't just any school; it was considered one of the best universities in the country! I was out of town one day and I thought about how awesome of an opportunity he had to do something that his family couldn't do when we were his age. I just looked out the window while driving my car and tears just began to fall. I was so happy! That's what you call a "Man! God did it" moment! B Disciplined because you may become the standard for those boys and men around you. Your life will be the better for it!

CHAPTER 8

B Confident

I pride myself on trying to look good and presentable at all times. However, this has not always been the case. I used to be one of those guys that only wanted to put on a jersey and some Air Force 1's and I thought I was good. I guess I mirrored a lot of the athletes and hip hop artists. I owned a lot of basketball jerseys and would buy another one every chance I got. But then the NBA changed its dress code in 2005 and that made me want to change mine. I started caring about the way I would dress in 2008. There would be times I would walk in a men's department store and go straight to the suit section. I would grab around 4-5 suits at a time and lay them out on the table. A salesman would come and offer assistance but I would decline his offer. They probably saw me grabbing the suits and thought they would be able to make a nice commission. What they didn't know was that I didn't have any money! I would be broke and all I had in my pocket was lint and a lot of it. If the lint was a symbol of finances, then I was balling out of control! After I picked the suits, I would go grab shirts, ties, socks, belts and shoes! I would just have it all laid out. There were even a couple of times when a customer would walk by and say, "Oh wow! I like that! You have a good fashion eye!" At that time, I did not know that God was going to use this skill and talent to birth a business for me and my family down the line.

After I put all the sets together, I would feel a sense of joy bubbling up in my spirit. To me, that was like therapy; like my oasis. You may have a hard time believing that I get this geeked from picking out clothes. But I really do! Once I put all the sets together, I would leave them there and walk out! Although I couldn't afford them, I would hope that someone else would walk by and purchase them before the salesman would come by and put everything back on the racks and shelves. It gave me a sense of gratification that someone thought my creation was nice enough to purchase! A couple of times that's exactly what happened. People would ask me if they could purchase the sets since I wasn't. To me, it didn't matter who bought them. It just felt great that someone liked my creation enough to purchase it.

All men love gratification and all men want to hear they are doing a great job; positive words of affirmation stimulate a man's self-worth. It really helps a man's self-esteem. In a society where men can sometimes find it tough to get gratification, it is important that they get it. Let's look at two families that have a husband, wife, and kids. Both have a husband that comes home from a hard day's work. Now one household has a husband that comes home and is greeted by cheers, letting him know that he is the man and that the family is blessed because of him! The wife and kids are both jumping up and down, letting him know how happy they are to have the man of the house home. Now the house is even more blessed because the husband just walked in! Now that man could have had a terrible day at work, but because of the gratification and cheers he received from the time he got home, he forgot all about his day and now his chest is sticking out from New York to California because he is celebrated by his family.

Now let's shift to the second household. The husband comes home from the same long day of work. But instead of the cheers, he comes home to complaints! The wife is complaining; the kids are caught up on their mobile devices and don't even notice dad is home! I know they both may seem a little far-fetched, but they both happen so often in our society. If you are a wife reading this book, I ask you to step back and take an inventory of the gratification your husband is getting or not getting when he is at home or for anything else he does. This may be a good time to put this book down and just go tell him, "Thank You!" Thank him for his efforts, accomplishments and his hard work! Think of something you can thank him for and let him know! Maybe you can have the kids write a thank you card or something for him. Do something to show him your gratitude for the job he is doing. Ladies, let me tell you, that will turn your man from Clark Kent to Superman! It doesn't have to be anything big, just something that shows him he is appreciated. We may not want to admit it, but men love it!

It is a great idea to do it every so often. Make it a point in life to have an occasional "Dad's Appreciation Day" on a day other than Father's Day.

Speaking and interacting with men has not always been something I've felt comfortable doing! It's amazing how God will take one of the biggest struggles of your childhood and use it as part of your purpose! When you are speaking with men and women, make sure you are looking them in the eyes. It is a sign of respect that lets them know you are listening to them. That was a big challenge for me. If I was in a room full of men, I felt out of place. Even if they were talking about something, I could possibly relate to like women or sports. I always felt like I didn't have a right to be in the conversation because I didn't grow up around a lot of men. It just seemed like I felt more comfortable talking in a women's setting than in a men's setting. It was probably easier for me because of the relationship I had with my mom and my sisters. My older brothers left home and my young brothers were a little too young, so my sisters were around my age group and that made it okay for me to talk to them. I never just considered my mom to be just my mom. Especially as I grew older, we would laugh and talk just like two old friends. We would have some disagreements like two old friends as well. That was the beauty of our relationship.

I believe men who struggle in this area will try just as hard to be accepted by men. This explains why I always felt that if my friends and I went out and they didn't have the funds to party and drink or ride, I would make sure they would be able to still go and I would take care of what they needed. If they needed money to get in the club, I had them. If they didn't have drink money, I had them. If they didn't have a ride, I picked them up. I just wanted to be accepted and I felt like this was a way to show them. But when the lights come on and the music stops, I was the one left wondering what to do next. I left unfulfilled and with an empty pocket. Not to mention, a super bad headache! Sometimes I can't help but wonder what or where I would be if I had just taken another road instead of the road I traveled. How much further would I be or how much more successful would I be? Then I quickly realize the road I am on is the road God designed for me and me alone.

I had to go this route to get to where God has me now. In this journey called purpose, only God can allow you to detour here and there during your journey. However, He will make sure that when the dust clears, you are still on the path He designed for you from the beginning. Who wouldn't love a father like that! Now I welcome a room full of men! As a matter of fact, I get goose bumps!

I remember in June 2009. I had a chance to travel to Dallas, Texas and attend my very first Men's Conference at The Potter's House where Bishop TD Jakes is the Pastor. I was so excited! I even had my work supervisor go with me! I had never been in a room that big with nothing but men and I felt right at home! I felt like I belonged there. If I would have done it in my early to mid-20's, I would have felt a little out of place. But I was in my 30's and God had delivered me from some things, so I was able to feel right at home. The conference was three days long and in the last Saturday session, Bishop Jakes had us get in circles of 10. He told each of us to share something from the heart about manhood. I went first! Again, normally this is something I would never have been able to do in the past! But because I had been delivered, I was locked and loaded and I delivered! That helped the rest of the men in the circle share their stories as well! I was even able to stay in contact with some of the men after the conference.

I believe men need men to talk to, strengthen each other and just be able to relate to. Without it, men tend to keep things inside, which can cause them to almost lose their mind. Men, if you don't have another man you can talk to, I suggest that you pray and ask God to lead and guide you to someone that you can confide in and who can help hold you accountable for your actions. Men desperately need that because when they have it, life is a lot easier. You have to make sure, however, that you confide in someone who is going to be honest with you! Someone who will be in your cheering corner when you are right, but not afraid to let you know when you are wrong with either. A lot of men feel like they can't go against a "guy code" and tell them something that they may not want to hear, but a real man has to be willing to hear the truth and get upset hearing it. And if you can't hear it or if you are not willing to tell it, then maybe that's not someone you should consider being a real friend.

So many men suffer in silence because they have no one to talk to. Society has tried to paint a picture that women talk and men just keep silent. When you do come across a man that speaks or talks a lot, his manhood is questioned! Men don't realize the power they have in their mouth by just speaking. The Bible says that life and death are in the power of the tongue! In order for you to speak life, you have to open your mouth! Years ago, when my wife and I had just gotten married, I was at work and my mother-in-law came over to check on her. She didn't like how my wife looked so she immediately called me and I left work to come and check on her. I was on the train and the first person I thought to call was my Pastor and she didn't answer! As I began to dial another number, God spoke to me and said, "Hang that phone up! As a man and a husband, you are going to have to deal with and handle this yourself!" See, this wasn't an ordinary sickness; it was spiritual warfare! Spiritual warfare is real and should not be taken lightly! The best way to fight spiritual warfare is with prayer! As I was on my way home, I have to admit I was afraid. But the more I talked to God, the more my fear turned into anger! I finally made it home and I didn't even get in the door good before I opened my mouth! It was like fire came out! I didn't even know I had a prayer life like that, but I knew that I had to do what I had to do! I realized and understood that the power was in my mouth and I had to open it!

Unfortunately, this was not the case 20 years earlier. My opening my mouth had gotten me and the people I was with in trouble! I may have been 8 or 9 and I was in the country with my family. My great uncle decided to take the boys fishing. We were super excited! We loaded up in the Cadillac and he took us to this area of acres and acres of land. On this land was a huge pond that was loaded with fish! You could literally see the fish in the pond! I mean hundreds and hundreds of fish! My uncle threw his rod in and he immediately got a bite. Then another bite and another bite! We were there maybe 30 minutes and had like 8 nice sized catfish that we were planning to eat later that night. Suddenly, 2 gentlemen pull up in a pickup truck and asked us what we were doing. Our uncle told us he was taking us fishing, but what he didn't tell us was that he was taking us fishing on someone's private property! The owners of this property caught us fishing on their property, which was illegal! Not only that, we had planned on catching their fish, taking them and cooking them for ourselves, which was stealing, which was also illegal! The owners were just asking us to leave. They didn't know we had already caught 8 nice sized fish! Until I opened my mouth to my uncle in front of the owners and said, "Unc, what about these in the buckets? Do we still get to keep them or do we have to put them back?" If looks could kill and if he could have gotten away with it, I probably would have been dead! So because of opening my mouth when I shouldn't have, we missed out on our catfish dinner! We get back to the house and my uncle told my mom how upset he was because I had opened my big mouth and now that catfish that my uncle had already skinned, battered and fried in his mind was just a dream! I remember him telling my mom what I had done and me feeling bad that my mouth had caused the family to go without! Granted, we should NOT have been there in the first place, but as a young man, I didn't think or realize that! It really made me sad that my family had missed out on an opportunity because I opened my mouth even though it wasn't my fault.

That's how life can do you if you choose to allow yourself to feel that way. Did I know better? No, I didn't! I am just glad that the situation didn't allow me to spend the rest of my life in silence! If you have ever had the chance to go to a movie in a movie theatre, you have heard the saying, "Silence is golden." But that isn't always the case! There are times when you have to be willing to open up your mouth and say something! If you are reading this and you have been holding something in for far too long and it has done nothing but cause you misery, I would like to recommend that you say something! You may need to tell a family member or someone else. Please don't suffer in silence! Say something and allow your saying something to help you get delivered!

Purpose is something that I have not always felt I had. There was a time in my life when I felt that where I was in life was the best it was going to be. I am so glad that God wouldn't allow me to stay there, but He pushed me into something more! I have been working at the same place for 21 years, but it took me 17 years to really understand that there was more for me. Where I was and what I had gone through was all God's way of preparing me for what was to come. But this route was necessary. I had to learn something. Well actually, I had to learn a lot! My 21 years in healthcare allowed me to see and experience a lot. I meet a lot of great people and not so great people. Even with that, it was still a part of my preparation. Not to mention, I had a lot of growing and maturing to do. There is nothing worse than an immature grown man.

B Confident enough to acknowledge someone else's God purpose and celebrate them when they walk in it.

Unfortunately, that was me for so many years. If I wasn't rude, I was loud. If I wasn't loud, I was mean! I am so glad that I didn't try to write this book some years ago because people probably would have looked at me as the author and thought I needed to be reading some self-help books myself!

But eventually, I grew and became a much better person. It wasn't an overnight experience, but once I made up my mind to make changes I did. I only began to make the changes once I knew that the state I was in wasn't working. So slowly but surely, I started evolving and becoming a better person. When I started working at the hospital, I was a young man, but I acted more like a young boy until I eventually became a man. I endured a lot of growing pains during this process, but I was focused on being better. Any real man knows that once he makes up his mind to be and do better, he can't be stopped! It's in a man's DNA that once he decides on something, it is full steam ahead! The key for a man is to decide and that may not be easy! Once we decide, we are held accountable for the decision we make. This can be good or bad. For instance, if a husband makes the decision to cheat on his wife and he gets caught, he then jeopardizes losing his family and having his world turned upside down, all because of his decision. The same holds true for the man who chooses to drink and drive, gets pulled over by police and arrested for DUI. Being arrested for a DUI is a very trying and expensive ordeal (getting out of jail on bond to paying lawyer fees). Not to mention the extra financial burden that it's going to put on his family.

In today's society, nobody has money to waste. But let's just say they take those same two scenarios and they do the opposite.

They decide not to cheat on their wife and not to drink and drive; saving themselves and their families a terrible headache! Men, if you are married and/or have kids, know your decisions don't just affect you, they affect your family too. So let that help you when you are trying to decide whether the choice you are about to make is going to help or hurt your family.

In the Bible, the first chapter of the book of Joshua says that God told Joshua to be strong and courageous. A lot of men today aren't showing their courageousness or their strength. Our men are trading in courage and strength for fame and fortune. Don't get me wrong, there is nothing wrong with fame and/or fortune if you know how to handle it in its proper perspective. The Bible also says, "What profit a man to gain the whole world and lose his soul." (Mark 8:36) (KJV) How sad is it for a man to gain so much but receive nothing! The life of a man can have its struggles, but in order to overcome those struggles, you have to make up your mind to be strong and courageous. Will you get some bumps and bruises? Yes, you will. But if you hang in there and keep fighting the good fight, victory is guaranteed! You will come out of it!

Every man loves the thrill of victory. Think about the victories that you may have accomplished thus far in your life and then think about the times it took you to be strong and courageous to make it. You probably didn't think you were going to make it and everything on the inside of you probably wanted to throw your hands up and quit. But then a still soft voice comes and says,

"Keep going. Don't stop. You are closer than you think. Hang in there. Be strong and courageous. Right on the other side is the victory!"

Think about what would have happened had Joshua quit. He would have never been able to lead the people of Israel to the land of milk and honey; which was called the Promised Land! Do you have a promised land? If so, are you walking in your strength and courage to get to it or have you decided that it's not for you? Are you forfeiting your promise? You may be tired, frustrated and even a little weary, but I cannot stress enough the importance of the push! Keep pushing! The easiest thing to do in this world is quit! Think about it, it takes no effort at all to quit! The urge to quit usually comes right when you are close; so close you can reach for it! But you decide to quit only to see that if you would have just kept going a little more, you would have finished! I have done this so many times. Take when I first started running for instance, focusing on getting myself in shape. I would run and set a goal for one mile. I would start off good. I would be proud of myself in the beginning, only to get close to my goal and decide to quit. I would look at my watch that kept track of my running and be devastated that I was so close to reaching my goal, only to quit right before the achievement!

If you have something you are trying to accomplish, I want to encourage you not to quit! Maybe you are wanting to lose weight or get a degree. Maybe you want to be a better husband or father and you are so close to victory. Please don't quit!

Maybe me writing and you reading this book is your sign to keep running! You can't see the finish line, but it's closer than you think. You may think things aren't going to turn around in your household or your marriage and you want to quit. Don't do it! Can you hear me? DON'T QUIT!

Hang on and catch your breath if need be, but don't quit! Remember your kids are watching you! As they grow up and have their own trials and tribulations, they want to be able to have a point of reference! Let that be you, their dad! Let them see that you didn't quit and know that they can't either. But if you do quit, you will be known as a quitter and they will think it's okay for them to be one too!

There was a movie that came out some years ago called "The Help". The movie was a story about black maids in the south during segregation days who had the courage to write a book about their experiences while being maids. Personally, I thought the movie was excellent, but what really grabbed my attention was the title. Unfortunately, that's a word that men hate to use. Men feel that if we use that word, we are unable to handle whatever we need help with, thus showing a sign of weakness. In the Bible, Jesus was out on the water and Peter asked if he could join Jesus on the water. Jesus allowed it, only to have Peter yell for help when he began to fall. Jesus was right there to help Peter and kept him from drowning. As men, we have to be willing to ask for help when we need it. Although we are built strong with broad shoulders (well some men anyway), we were not created to be able to carry things by ourselves. Think about the book of Genesis when God says it wasn't good for man to be alone, so He created a woman and He called her a helpmate! Even the Creator knew we would need help!

I am guilty of this. Thinking I can do it all on my own because I am a man! I got it! Men, be honest. Have you ever been doing something like changing a tire or lifting a heavy box and you were struggling? I mean really struggling! Like you are about to pass out!

Someone comes along and sees you struggling and asks you if you need help. You respond with, "Oh no, I got it!" Refusing to let your help do just that, help! There have been numerous times in my life as a young man and as a grown man when I needed help and didn't ask or accept it. All because I didn't think that was the manly thing to do. At the beginning of my marriage, my wife and I bumped heads quite a bit because she would be there, ready and willing to help and I would tell her that I had it. In reality, I was struggling like crazy and really needed the help! Men, understand that our biggest strength is being able to confess and share our weaknesses and the fact that we sometimes need help, whether it's needing help with something around the house or having a struggle with drugs or alcohol. Don't be ashamed to get what you need in order to be better. You may need help from a friend, confide in them about what's taking place in your life. Go and get the help you need! When I need help with a decision, I go to my two oldest brothers, Patrick and Gregg. They are both older and more experienced than me in certain areas. Plus, I know that no matter what I may need help with, they will not judge me nor will they look at me any different. They will give me the help I need and it will be sound advice!

My wife is also one that is there to assist when I need help. It took me a while to grasp that concept. Help is not a bad thing. In fact, it can be a very good thing if you embrace it. So if there is an area in your life that's a struggle and you need some help, don't let your pride get the best of you. Humble yourself and get what you need. Pray about it and ask God to be your helper. He will send you the help you need. He did it for Peter and He can do it for you. B Confident enough to acknowledge someone else's God purpose and celebrate them when they walk in it. You never diminish yourself when you do so, especially when you are affirming someone else's gifting and calling.

CHAPTER 9

B Coming

I believe most men will agree that the transition from boyhood to manhood is not easy. Since the beginning of time, mankind has had a bullseye on its chest, hoping for them to fail and not be the men that God has created them to be. The enemy has always had a direct intent to try to destroy men! In both the Old and New Testaments, there were times when there was a hit out on young men because the ones that wanted young boys killed knew they would eventually become men. Can you imagine this world without men being in it? Don't get me wrong, the things women do in this world are great! Some of my biggest influences in life have been women. But to think of this world existing without men is just crazy to me! When I look on TV today and see a man taking the life of another man, it hurts me to my core, because now that's one less man that we have in this country that could have possibly made a difference in today's society. But I wonder how much stronger men would be if we began to help and build each other up instead of fighting against one another. This can start in our childhood.

Let's do an exercise. Think about the last male you took time out to encourage and give them a sense of hope. Or better yet, think of all the men you may have come across today that you just looked at and never said anything to. You were close enough to speak and chose not to! You may have been on the elevator or on the train going into work with them and never said anything to them. It didn't have to be anything deep. Just acknowledge them being in your presence with a greeting such as, "What's up man?" or "Hello, how are you?" Some may think it sounds kind of corny, but who knows what that simple act of speaking can do for the man who receives it? Listen, speaking to, supporting or encouraging another man doesn't make you any less of a man. If anything, it should make you feel like more of a man. I would like to see another man have a good day because I know what it's like to be a man. I know that there are days that can be rough for a man. I know that the enemy would love to have all men gone. If he is married with kids, I know what it's like to have a family at home. So I am going to encourage you because it may be all the encouragement you receive today. So many times, I have been somewhere and come across a man or two and taken time out to thank him! I just thanked him for standing and being a man!

I wrote this book to help someone who may have gone through some of the same journeys I have gone through. I want to show them that they can make it if I was able to make it! Jesus told Peter that the enemy has need of thee, but He prayed that his faith failed not. And after he was converted, He told him to strengthen his brethren! That's my reason for writing this book; to strengthen a brother. Whether you are a young brother, a middle-aged brother or an older brother, it doesn't matter. I always like to tell young men that I have the privilege to speak to that the mistakes I made and the issues I went through I went through them so you don't have to. That's why God brought me to them. I can now share them with you and hopefully stop you from wanting to make the same mistakes I made. My prayer is for a man to be walking in Walmart and see my book, decide to purchase it, read it and realize he relates to it and seeks God to make the necessary changes in his life! Maybe a mother will see my book in Barnes and Noble and purchase and read it and see that her teenage son is going through the exact same things that I sent my mom through. But hopefully it gives her hope that he will come out of it.

If you are a married Man, make sure you do everything you can to be emotionally connected to your spouse. Too many marriages today are separated because they are weak in the emotional

> **My prayer is that my story will inspire you to B the Man God has called you to be.**

communication areas. You have to make sure you are not giving the enemy space to come in and try to divide what God has put together. Notice I said try, because if you stay grounded and focused on your garden (your wife) and till and care for it, she will blossom like you won't believe! Every gardener wants a garden that flourishes. Men, connect with your wife. If possible, make sure you seek God's wise counsel and go into battle and fight for your garden. Make sure you are not more focused on manicuring and developing another garden while your garden is being neglected with weeds growing all around it! I speak from experience. When you are working and focused on so many other things, sometimes the things closest to you can be disregarded or feel neglected. A garden is a gift from God. It is something that should be appreciated and taken care of. Can you imagine being so great in so many other areas but not in the area that is most important to God? That is your marriage. My marriage is not perfect, but as time went on, I realized that there were things I could do better to make my marriage better. Marriage is what you make it. After marriage, sometimes men can feel like the person we married was the wrong person. But we should treat the person like they are the right person until they become the right person!

In life, there has only been one perfect man, and that is Jesus Christ! His life was set for Him to die on purpose for the betterment of all mankind. So if you are looking to be perfect, stop it! You are fighting a losing battle. Now even though you can't be perfect, you can be consistent. If I can tell you anything, it is to be consistent! Be consistent in your prayer life and in your relationship with God! That has to be what your foundation is built upon.

Husbands, be consistent in being a Godly husband. Your prayers are dependent upon the way you treat and handle your wife. The Bible says it plain and clear, "Treat her as a weaker vessel or your prayers will be hindered." (1 Peter 3:7) (KJV) Notice it didn't say her prayers, but yours. Also, before you take a wife, make sure you have your life in order and know where you are going. Women like to be led and if you are not sure where you are going, it will be a struggle for them to follow you. Lastly, fathers, put forth a consistent effort to be the best father you can be, even if your father wasn't. You owe it to your child to give them your best. The only way to do that is to be consistent. I made a lot of mistakes in all of these areas and sometimes I still do. However, since I gave my life to Christ, they are not as bad as they used to be. Now, I learn from my mistakes and keep going. Why? Because I know He is with me. The blessing of it all is the fact that He is not only with me, but He is with you as well. Let God lead and direct your steps along your journey. As He does, encourage and share your journey with someone else.

Being self-centered is never good. A lot of my bad choices were made from a self- centered perspective, never really considering all parties involved. I only wanted to look out for myself, and when you are married with kids, that's not the kind of person you should want to be.

Although I know I still have a long way to go, I am so grateful to God for changing my life and allowing me to be the man, husband, and father I am today! I understand that everything that happened in my life (the good, bad and ugly) had to happen because it was all a part of my purpose. There were times, both in my boyhood and manhood, when I didn't think things would ever get better! But God! Look at me now! So because He saw fit to bring me out of my dark place in life, I accept my purpose driven assignment to reach back and pull my brothers (young and old) out! My prayer is that my story will inspire you to B the Man God has called you to be. Now go and make the world a better place!

ABOUT the AUTHOR

KEVIN D. BOUDREAUX, a man who is focused and destined to fulfill his Divine purpose and calling. Kevin is a successful entrepreneur. He is the owner and image consultant for B the Man Apparel and Accessories. B the Man was Kevin's first baby, so it holds a special place in his heart but he knew God had something more precious for him to birth, which is Mentoring Young Men. Following his passion, in September 2014 Kevin took a leap of faith and became a Certified Life Coach with the focus of Coaching Men and Young Men. Kevin feels if he shares his story with young men with proper guidance and mentorship it will keep them from making some of the same mistakes he made in life. Kevin's motto to young men is "I did it so you don't have to"! Kevin is driven, focused, and determined to achieve his mission which is to help young men find and fulfill their purpose in life. In 2018 Kevin has added "author" to his resume in the releasing of his first book B-Coming my journey from boyhood to manhood. It is Kevin hope that people will read his book and believe it matters not how they may start but that they can eventually become the man that God has created them to be. Kevin is married to his lovely wife Darla and they have 3 beautiful daughters Shariye, KeBria, and Shania.

www.ingramcontent.com/pod-product-compliance
Lightning Source LLC
Chambersburg PA
CBHW071315110426
42743CB00042B/2547